Karate Class

by Phoebe Marsh
illustrated by
Mary O'Keefe Young

MODERN CURRICULUM PRESS
Pearson Learning Group

Linn is going to karate class.

She loves it!

Linn has a karate outfit.
It looks like pajamas.
She puts it on.

Linn has a white belt.
She wants a black one
someday.

Some belts are yellow or blue.
There are brown ones too.
Black belts are for the best.

The best can chop wood.
They use bare hands.
Linn can not chop wood yet.

Linn takes her shoes off.

She bows to her teacher.

No one says a word.

Linn stretches.

She bows.

The bow means "I am ready."

They are going to begin.

Linn kicks and blocks.
She hops and chops.

She yells a karate yell.

But she is not mad.

The yell is part of karate.
Everyone has fun.

Linn bows again.

This bow means "Thank you."

Linn is quiet again.
Everyone is.

Linn bows to the teacher.
Everyone bows.
"Thank you for the class."
That is what this bow means.

Linn feels good.

She always does after karate.